RE THEY BUILT?

DAMS

Lynn M. Stone

Rourke Publishing LLC
Vero Beach, Florida 32964

www.rourkepublishing.com

PHOTO CREDITS:
Cover ©Corel; pages 18, 28 ©AP/Wide World; pages 30, 31, 32 ©Dynamic Designs; page 40 ©AP; pages 4, 7, 8, 10, 11, 15, 16, 21, 22, 24, 26, 35, 36, 39, 41, 43 courtesy of the U.S. Department of the Interior, Bureau of Reclamation.

EDITORIAL SERVICES:
Pamela Schroeder

ABOUT THE AUTHOR
Lynn Stone is the author of more than 400 children's books. He is a talented natural history photographer as well. Lynn, a former teacher, travels worldwide to photograph wildlife in its natural habitat.

Library of Congress Cataloging-in-Publication Data

Stone, Lynn M.
    Dams / Lynn M. Stone
        p. cm. — (How are they built?)
    Includes bibliographical references and index.
    Summary: Describes different kinds of dams, how and why they are built, and their effects on the environment.
    ISBN 1-58952-136-6
        1. Dams—Juvenile literature. [1. Dams.] I. Title

TC540 .S79 2001   2001041649
627'.8 21

Printed In The USA

TABLE OF CONTENTS

Dams .5

History of Dams 19

Who Builds Dams? 23

Kinds of Dams 29

Dams vs. Nature 33

Building Dams. 37

Important Dams 44

Glossary 46

Index 48

Further Reading/Websites 48

Dams block the flow of rivers and form wide artificial lakes, or reservoirs.

DAMS

Give beavers credit for the first dams. But give people credit for taking the art of dam building to new heights. While beaver dams haven't changed over the years, the dams constructed by human **engineers** have—in big ways!

Modern dams are stronger and bigger than ever. In fact, dams are the largest structures ever built, except for the Great Wall of China. The artificial lakes, or **reservoirs**, that form behind the largest dams hold trillions of cubic feet of water!

Dams may be simple or complex. They may serve one purpose or many. And they can be built of one or more materials. But dams of all types and sizes have the same common goal—to block a river's flow. Basically, dams are barriers to the natural flow of a river or stream.

Many small streams feed a river. These streams feed a river even when a dam is in place. Finding its path blocked by a dam, the river rises, becomes deeper, and spreads out. This process creates a new, deeper, wider body of water—the reservoir—behind the dam. Some of the largest dams form lakes more than 100 miles (162 km) long.

Dams are often built in remote country, where their reservoirs will not flood villages and farms.

Being able to water crops even in dry seasons is an important benefit of dams.

Dams also create new jobs for people who live in that area.

Creating big dams and reservoirs is expensive. Are dams worth the money? Yes, no, and maybe. Dams do good things for people. Yet for every benefit a dam provides, **critics** can find a problem caused by the same dam. Most people, however, agree that some dams are good while others are, at best, **controversial**.

The benefits of dams are many. One benefit is **irrigation**. Remember, many rivers in dry parts of the world, including the American Southwest, are dry at some times of the year. Constructing a dam and creating a reservoir provides water for crops and farm animals, even during dry seasons. Farmers take water from the reservoir through pipes and canals.

Huge turbines and generators are used to produce hydroelectric power—electricity made from the energy of falling water.

Another major benefit of dams is **hydroelectric** power. This is electricity made by the force of falling water. Many modern dams create artificial waterfalls with huge force. The falling water powers machines called **turbines**. Together with **generators**, it produces electricity for millions of people in North America.

*Dams that produce electricity have huge engine rooms
built into their structure.*

Some dams are for flood control. After a heavy rain or snowmelt, a river can overflow its banks and flow through cities and farmland. Because of the dam's reservoir, the river's ability to cause flood damage and destroy lives is limited. For example, as the spring snowmelt begins, dam controllers or operators will begin to release water from the reservoir. This now leaves room in the reservoir to hold the additional water from the snowmelt and prevent flooding. Modern dams can control water levels through a system of gates and **spillways**. By changing the reservoir water level, a dam can also change the level of water downstream, below the dam. Water level manipulation can be a good thing. Downstream, for example, it can provide a steady source of water for boaters and wildlife.

Another benefit of dams is recreation. Many North American reservoirs have become favorite spots for sailing, power boating, windsurfing, fishing, and swimming. Lake Mead , the huge lake created by the Hoover Dam, is a national recreation area visited by millions of people each year. The Hoover Dam stands 700 feet (213 m) tall. It is one of the most visited dams in the world.

The controversial side of dams comes from what they are designed to do. By their nature, dams change landscapes. Whether or not someone likes the way a dam looks isn't the issue. The landscapes above and below a dam are issues. The health of the river **ecosystem** is another issue.

When a dam backs a river upstream, the reservoir spreads over the landscape. Engineers who design dams have a good idea about where the reservoir will go. The size of a new reservoir doesn't come as a surprise. The question is whether the reservoir is better for the people and the ecosystem than the dry land it replaced. In Africa, the Kariba Dam forced 30,000 tribespeople to move. The Glen Canyon Dam in Arizona flooded a scenic canyon and its Indian **artifacts**. The Aswan High Dam in Egypt caused some artifacts to be buried underwater. In China, the Three Gorges Dam is creating even bigger controversies.

The problem occurs when a government decides to build a dam and people must move to accommodate the area that will be flooded. How would you react if you were asked to relocate your home or town?

Workers look over plans of the Three Gorges dam.

The Three Gorges is a huge dam. When it is
finished in 2009, it will reach more than 1 mile (1.6 km)
across the Yangtze River. It will stand 600 feet (183 m)
above the valley, and it will produce more electric
power than any dam in the world. But the Three Gorges
will move more than 1 million Chinese from their homes
along the Yangtze's banks. It is also drowning beautiful
canyons, ancient temples, and villages. It may wipe out
the Yangtze River dolphin and, at the same time,
become a huge trap for **pollutants**.

Dams make it difficult if not impossible for fish to migrate.

Wild animals often don't survive when their environments are changed. A flowing river and its wetlands are a different kind of ecosystem than a reservoir. And the dam itself can cause major problems for **migrating** fish. Some dams have "fish ladders", a series of pools that migrating fish can use to move over the dam. Unfortunately, fish ladders only work in certain areas. Pacific salmon and steelhead trout in the dammed rivers of the Northwest are beginning to disappear. Eighteenth-and nineteenth-century dams in New England almost wiped out the Atlantic salmon.

Rivers carry mud and fine particles called **silt**. During floods, rivers dump some of their silt on "bottomland," the fertile lowlands along river valleys. Silt helps keep bottomlands fertile. But rivers that flow into reservoirs leave most of their silt in the reservoir. That means bottomlands become less fertile. The famous Aswan High Dam produces huge amounts of electricity for Egypt. But the Nile River no longer leaves silt on Egyptian bottomlands. Farmers have to use about 1 million tons (909,000 metric tons) of factory fertilizer instead.

Like any human-made structures, dams are not perfect. A dam that does not work the way it is supposed to can be dangerous. There are many stories of dams that failed. One of the most well known in the United States is the South Fork Dam. The South Fork Dam was built of clay, boulders, and dirt. In 1889 it failed and sent a 40-foot (12-m) wave into Johnstown, Pennsylvania. At least 2,209 people were killed. More recently, in 1963, a landslide poured into the reservoir behind the dam at Vaiont, Italy. Water displaced by the slide rushed over the dam and into the valley below. More than 2,000 people died. In this case, the dam didn't fail, but the dam's designers had never thought a landslide could happen.

Townspeople stand amid the wreckage caused by the Johnstown Flood in 1889.

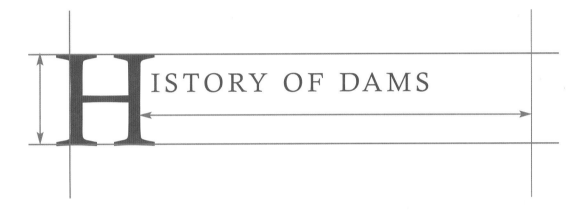

HISTORY OF DAMS

The earliest human-made dams were much like those beavers build, made of brush, rock, and mud. The ponds created by those dams gave their builders a steady source of water and fish.

Using stone and banks of earth, builders learned to block entire rivers with their dams. The earliest known dam, across the Nile River, was built about 5,000 years ago. The reservoir from the dam allowed farmers to move water into their fields. The oldest dam still used is a 3,300-year-old structure in Syria.

The Romans, known for their engineering, built many dams of cut stone throughout their empire. Some of those dams, built more than 2,000 years ago, are still in use.

The first dam in the United States was probably one built in South Berwick, Maine, in 1634. Like later dams in New England, the Berwick dam was used to power a **grist** mill. Water flowing through a spillway powered water wheels. The wheels, in turn, were connected to moving parts that caused millstones to grind grain.

*Dams have been used for 5,000 years to create lakes,
irrigate dry fields, and produce power.*

Not long after the Berwick dam was built in Maine, the French built a 115-foot (35-m) high dam near Toulouse, France. It was the world's tallest dam for 150 years. Dams became more important as engineers learned more about how dams could control rivers and produce power for factories. William Rankine, a Scottish engineer, used math and science in dam designs in 1870. Suddenly, the building of dams entered a new, modern era, far more scientific than the old.

The control center of a modern dam is filled with operating and monitoring equipment.

WHO BUILDS DAMS?

Dams are too expensive and affect too many people to be built by individuals. That usually leaves the building of dams to governments. In the United States, one dam builder is the Bureau of Reclamation. The Army Corp of Engineers, another government agency, also builds dams in the United States.

*Another load of concrete is shuttled by a hoist for the
Hungry Horse Dam in Montana.*

When government officials agree a dam is needed, even if the idea is not popular, the government undertakes the project. Planning for a dam can take years because of the often controversial nature of such projects. Once the engineers have completed their designs, the construction of the dam begins using one or more construction companies.

Planning and supervising dam construction is in the hands of engineers. The engineers' biggest tasks are to decide what shape the dam will be and what materials to use.

Engineers also have to decide exactly where the dam will be built. They need to find the right kind of soil or rock foundation. Engineers choose what kind of dam based on where the dam will be and what it is used for. A dam for hydroelectric power needs to be high. Height creates a taller waterfall with more force and more energy.

Engineers are involved with the maintenance of dams as well as with their planning and construction.

Engineers find answers using **geological** surveys, computers, and scale-size models. After dams are built, engineers continue to help maintain them. Dams can crack, leak, and even self-destruct if they are not taken care of. In 1995 a spillway gate on the Folsom Dam in California broke. Forty percent of Folsom Lake poured through the gate before it was fixed. Fortunately, flood damage was limited, but the dam needed $20 million in repairs. Now, with rope-climbing skills, engineers check hard-to-reach spillway gates on Folsom and other dams. The famous Johnstown Flood happened because the spillway of the South Fork Dam became clogged with trees and other debris. As the river—and the reservoir—rose with heavy rainfall, the spillway could not lower the reservoir level. When water washed over the earthen dam, it fell apart.

The removal of old dams allows rivers to flow freely and fish to migrate up and down the river.

Sometimes engineers suggest that an old dam be removed rather than repaired. In 1999 the first state that had a dam, Maine, became the first to remove a dam for environmental reasons. The old Edwards Dam, built in 1837 across the Kennebec River, was removed to help migrating fish. In the first 18 months after the Edwards Dam was removed, more than 40 more small dams in the United States were removed.

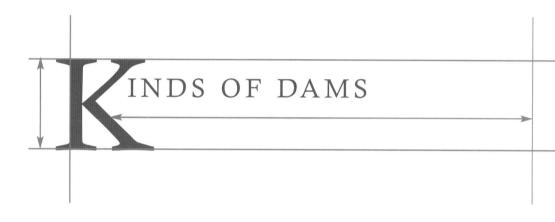

KINDS OF DAMS

Dams are named for the material with which they are made. Masonry dams are made of cut stones or concrete. Embankment dams are built of earth, loose rocks, gravel, sand, or types of soil, such as clay. Embankment dams are the oldest and simplest type. Some dams use both masonry and earth. A few small dams are made with rocks and timbers.

Embankment dams that are filled with materials from the ground are earth-fill dams. The center of an earth-fill dam is a waterproof core made from clay or concrete. The outer layer of an earth-fill dam is made of protective rock called **riprap**.

Rock-fill embankment dams are built of rocks and boulders. They're covered with concrete, steel, clay, or **asphalt** on the upstream side, where the river meets the dam. The covering makes the dam waterproof.

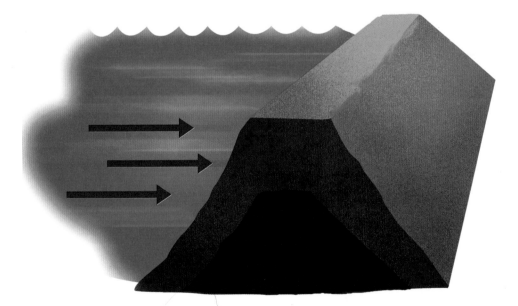

Water presses against an embankment dam, but the dam's weight, pushing into the ground, easily resists the water's pressure on it.

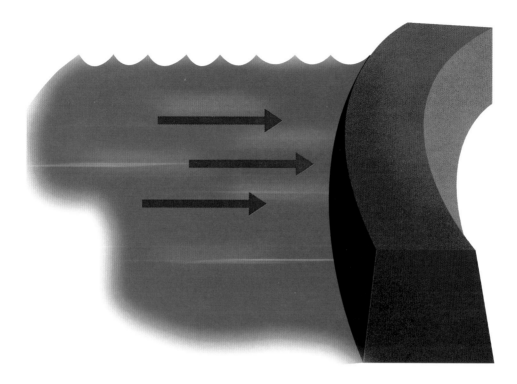

The arch dam is named for its archlike curve, the shape of which helps transfer the water pressure from the arch to the solid rock of the canyon walls.

Masonry dams are named by their shape and style. Gravity dams, like the Grand Coulee Dam in Washington, are the mightiest of dams. Concrete arch dams are built in narrow canyons. Arch dams curve toward the flow of the river. Concrete arch dams, first used in the 1950s, require far less concrete than gravity dams of the same length.

Buttress dams may be flat or curved. In either case, they are made of **reinforced concrete**. They are built in broad valleys where wide dams are required. Buttresses are vertical supports that are built against the dam's dry, downstream face.

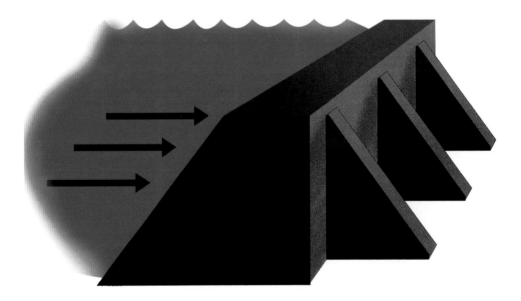

Buttress dams are reinforced by vertical support structures on the down-stream face of the dam. Like most dams, buttress dams are wider at their base.

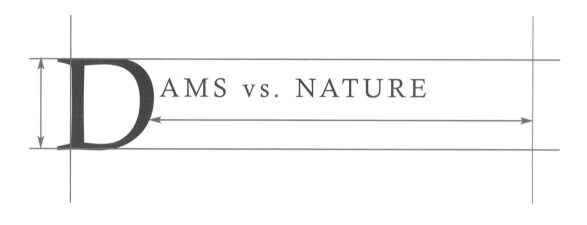DAMS vs. NATURE

Engineers build dams to control water. However, it is the nature of water to go over, through, past, under, or over anything in its way. Engineers and rivers play a high-stakes game of cat and mouse. It's a game that engineers cannot afford to lose. Engineers try to build dams that are watertight and can stand up to the force of water.

Water pressure increases with depth. That's why a dam's lower face is thicker than its upper. Think about the Hoover Dam. It would look triangle-shaped if you could cut it in half. It stands 700 feet (213 m) tall and has a 660-foot (201-m) thick base that becomes narrower toward the top of the dam.

Gravity and buttress dams transfer the water's force downward to the dam's foundation. Embankment dams, too, depend on their bulk and weight to resist the push of water. With arch dams, the water's force is transferred along the arch to the canyon walls.

Hoover Dam is 660 feet thick at its base.

The Flaming Gorge Dam on the Green River was built
after many years of studies and planning.

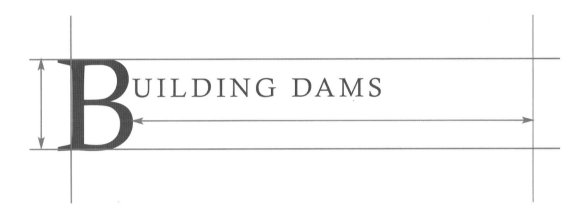

BUILDING DAMS

Dam builders have a very difficult and important job. Dam building requires careful planning and design. **Geologists** and engineers work together to study the earth on which the dam will be built. The dam will need a solid foundation. Engineers need to know how large an area the reservoir will flood, once the dam is built.

The studies require **topographical** maps and **borings** into the ground at the dam site. A model of the dam and the area it will flood are helpful to the designers. With the help of computers, engineers can predict how the real landscape will be affected by the dam.

The area to be flooded creates a different kind of challenge for dam builders. Property has to be bought. Homes, towns and their people may have to be moved.

Engineers have to figure out how much silt and mud will be carried into the reservoir and at what rate. These predictions help planners know how long the reservoir will be useful for holding water. As silt builds up, a reservoir is able to hold less and less water.

Get a plastic cup and fill it to the top with water. Pour the water into a measuring cup. Place several stones in the bottom of the cup. Now pour the water back into the glass and you will see that the cup holds less water. Silt and mud work the same way, displacing water in a reservoir.

The construction of a dam begins with a dam's foundation. Foundation work requires a dry riverbed, so engineers have to re-route the river, or part of it, away from the dam site. One way to re-route the river is with **cofferdams**. Cofferdams are small, temporary dams that re-route all or part of the river. For cofferdams to work, engineers have to make a new **channel**. Sometimes that is a tunnel they bore through rock. The Hoover Dam was built after workers re-routed the Colorado River into tunnels blasted through the rock walls of Black Canyon on the Arizona-Nevada border.

Bulldozers and other earth-moving equipment need a dry riverbed to begin construction of a dam.

Steel rods called rebar are used to make concrete stronger.

Sometimes a river is re-routed into a **diversion** channel. It took workers at the huge Itaipu Dam site in South America nearly three years just to build a diversion channel for the Parana River.

In a dry riverbed, construction can begin on the dam's foundation. A dam foundation is made of concrete poured into a trench cut in bedrock. Steel rods bored in the bedrock help tie the concrete to the rock. The foundation has to be watertight, so it may go 100 feet (30 m) underground to stay under the water. Workers force grout, a liquid cement, into the holes where the steel rods were set. The grout seals cracks.

Embankment dams have a core of watertight material, like clay or concrete. Earth-moving equipment builds up the sides of the embankment dam around the core. More machines press the earth of the dam to make it firm. Riprap is placed on the upstream face of the dam.

A concrete dam is built up with layers of poured concrete. Two concrete factories were built at the site when the Hoover Dam was built in the 1930s. Concrete is moved with trucks, hoists, and cranes. On some dams, concrete is poured on framework. On others, concrete blocks are poured, then moved into place within the dam.

Adding the finishing touches to the top of Hoover Dam.

A dam may look simple from the outside. But some dams are more than solid structures. They have pipes and passages within. **Penstocks**, for example, are tunnels, sometimes 20 feet (6 m) across. Water from the dam reservoir is routed through penstocks toward the turbines of hydroelectric dams. Screens above the penstocks keep fish and debris from reaching the tunnel and turbines.

Other tunnels, called scouring galleries, are built into some dams. Through water pressure, scouring galleries are designed to remove silt. Silt can clog water passages in the dam.

Engineers don't want the reservoir to overflow the dam. Overflows can damage any dam, but they can destroy an earthen dam. Spillways are the dam's safety valves. They are used to release water when needed. Some spillways have huge gates. They control water in the reservoir like your faucet controls water flowing into a sink. How much water is released from a dam, and when it is released, can be controversial, however.

*Fish screens like the one shown here keep fish
from being sucked into the dam turbines.*

Another important part in the construction of hydroelectric dams is the powerhouse. The equipment that makes electricity is in the powerhouse. Engineers place powerhouses as far below the reservoir water level as they can. The further the water falls, the more force it brings to the power equipment. The greater the force, the more power the station can produce.

IMPORTANT DAMS

Grand Coulee, Columbia River, Washington. A concrete gravity dam, the Grand Coulee was completed in 1942. It is still the largest dam in the United States and one of the world's largest concrete structures. It contains enough concrete to build a highway across America!

Hoover Dam, Colorado River, Nevada and Arizona. The Hoover Dam's Lake Meade is the largest human-made reservoir in the USA. Hoover Dam is the second highest dam (700 feet, 213 m) in the country. It's a concrete gravity dam with a curve.

Tarbela Dam, Indus River, Pakistan. The Tarbela is not the highest or longest dam in the world, but it's one of the biggest. This is an embankment dam of earth and rock more than 1 1/2 miles (2.4 km) long.

Kariba Dam, Zambezi River, Zambia. The Kariba is a concrete arch dam, 420 feet (128 m) high. Finished in 1959, it is a major producer of electricity. Lake Kariba, 174 miles (278 km) long, stretches behind the dam.

Daniel Johnson Dam, Quebec. This dam has 14 buttresses linked by arches and two more large buttresses in the middle. It's over 700 feet (213 m) high and nearly 1 mile (1.6 km) long. Finished in 1968, it's the largest of its type in the world.

Three Gorges Dam, Yangtze River, China. When it's completed in 2009, Three Gorges will be one of the most formidable structures on Earth—and the largest hydroelectric producer. The lake behind the dam will stretch about 350 miles (560 km), the distance from Los Angeles to San Francisco. About 20,000 workers are laboring day and night to complete the dam.

Aswan High Dam, Nile River, Egypt. Built for Egypt by Soviet engineers between 1960-1970, the Aswan was designed for flood control, irrigation, and hydroelectric power. The dam increased Egypt's ability to create power by six! The Aswan's Lake Nasser is one of the world's largest artificial lakes.

Ita Dam, Uruguai River, Brazil. Completed in 2000, the Ita is a 400-foot (122-m) high embankment dam of rock.

Itaipu Dam, Parana River, Brazil and Paraguay. Built between 1975-1991, Itaipu is the world's largest hydroelectric dam. But it will only be the largest until the Three Gorges Dam is completed in China. The amazing Itaipu is a mixture of masonry and embankment dam styles nearly 5 miles (8 km) long. The American Society of Civil Engineers named it one of the Seven Wonders of the Modern World.

GLOSSARY

artifact (AHR teh fakt) — any product of a culture's artistic efforts

asphalt (AS fawlt) — a tar-like substance

boring (BOHR ing) — a hole in rock or soil created by a drill, or the act of drilling

buttress (BUH tris) — a vertical support

channel (CHAN el) — a passageway, especially for a river

cofferdam (KAWF er dam) — a structure to keep water out of an area that is normally submerged; a small, temporary dam

controversial (kahn tre VER shel) — causing debate or argument

critic (KRIT ik) — one who analyzes a situation and may find fault

diversion (dih VUR zhun) — that which distracts or removes from the original course

ecosystem (EE koh sis tem) — a complete, natural community of plants and animals

engineer (en jeh NEER) — one who uses science and math to the design of various structures

generator (JEN eh ray ter) — a machine which produces electricity

geological (jee eh LOJ ik el) — of or related to the Earth

geologist (jee AHL eh jist) — a scientist who studies the Earth

grist (GRIST) — grain for grinding

hydroelectric (hy droh ih LEK trik) — relating to electricity produced by water power

irrigation (ir eh GAY shen) — supplying water to crops by artificial means, such as by canals

migrating (MY grayt ing) — moving from one location to another

penstock (PEN stahk) — a tunnel through which water is routed from a reservoir to a turbine

pollutant (peh LOO tent) — that which pollutes, or makes soiled, such as some chemicals

reinforced concrete (ree in FORST KAHN kreet) — very strong concrete that has been poured on steel wires or rods

reservoir (REZ er vwahr) — an artificial lake

riprap (RIP rap) — a layer or wall of stones used to prevent erosion

silt (SILT) — tiny, loose grains or particles of rock, sand, and soil

spillway (SPIL way) — a passageway on a dam for excess water to be released

topographical (tahp eh GRAF ik al) — of or related to the natural surface features of an area

turbine (TUR bin) — a type of engine that works with water power

INDEX

buttresses 32

computers 27, 38

concrete 30, 31, 40, 41

construction 25, 39, 40

dam
  arch 31, 34
  earth-fill 30
  embankment 29, 30,
    34, 41
  gravity 31, 34
  masonry 29, 31

dam builders 37, 38

ecosystem 13, 14, 17

electricity 10, 17, 43

engineers 5, 14, 22, 25, 28,
  33, 37, 38, 39, 42, 43

farmers 9, 17, 20

fish 17, 28, 42

flood control 12

foundation 34, 37, 39, 40

Hoover Dam 13, 34, 39, 41

hydroelectric power 10, 25

irrigation 9

Johnstown Flood 18, 27

powerhouse 43

Rankine, William 22

reservoirs 6, 9, 12, 13, 14,
  17, 18, 20, 27, 37, 38,
  42, 43

riprap 30, 41

river 6, 12, 14, 17, 20,
  27, 30, 31, 22, 39, 40

rocks 19, 29, 30

silt 17, 38, 42

spillways 12, 20, 27, 43

waterfalls 10, 25

Further Reading:
Dunn, Andrew. *Dams.* Thomson Learning, 1993
Gresko, Marcia. *The Grand Coulee Dam.* Blackbirch, 1999

Websites to Visit:
www.pbs.org/wgbh/buildingbig/dam/basics
www.usbr.gov
www.usbr.gov/cdams/dams/glencanyon
www.hoover.dam.usbr.gov